A

The ^ 12 days of Christmas

Mike Bourton

To Samuel

Mike

Author/Illustrator: Mike Bourton

A CIP catalogues record of the publication is available from the British Library.

ISBN: 9781739859800
Publisher: The Casual Book Company www.casualbookcompany.com
Designer: Jack Bourton
Editor: Alison Grinter
Printer: Bleuprint Ltd

www.thecasualpoet.com

the casual book company

The 12 days of Christmas is the period in Christian theology that marks the span between the birth of Christ and the coming of the Three Wise Men. It begins on Christmas Day and runs through until January 6th. For most, however, it is also a Christmas carol which recounts the gifts received from 'their true love' during the 12 days of Christmas.

I tried to imagine what it would feel like, in our modern world, to actually receive those gifts. Not quite as jolly, as I am sure you find, as you read through the days. I hope it does not happen to you!

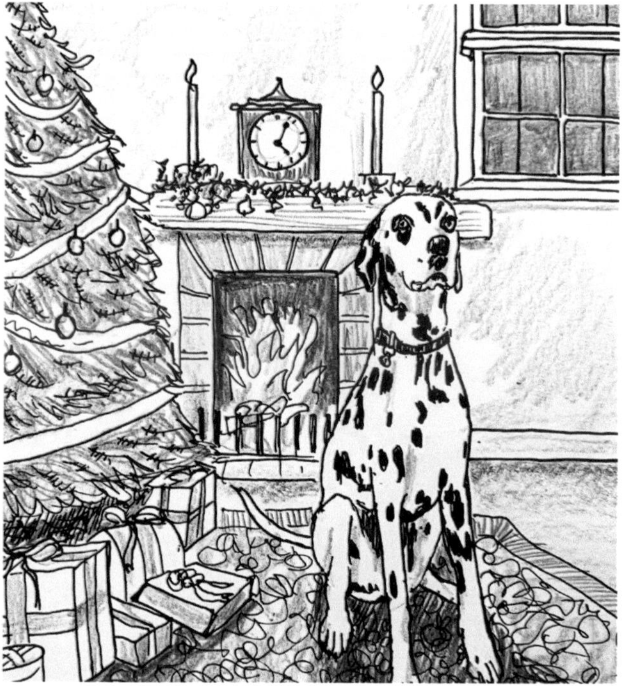

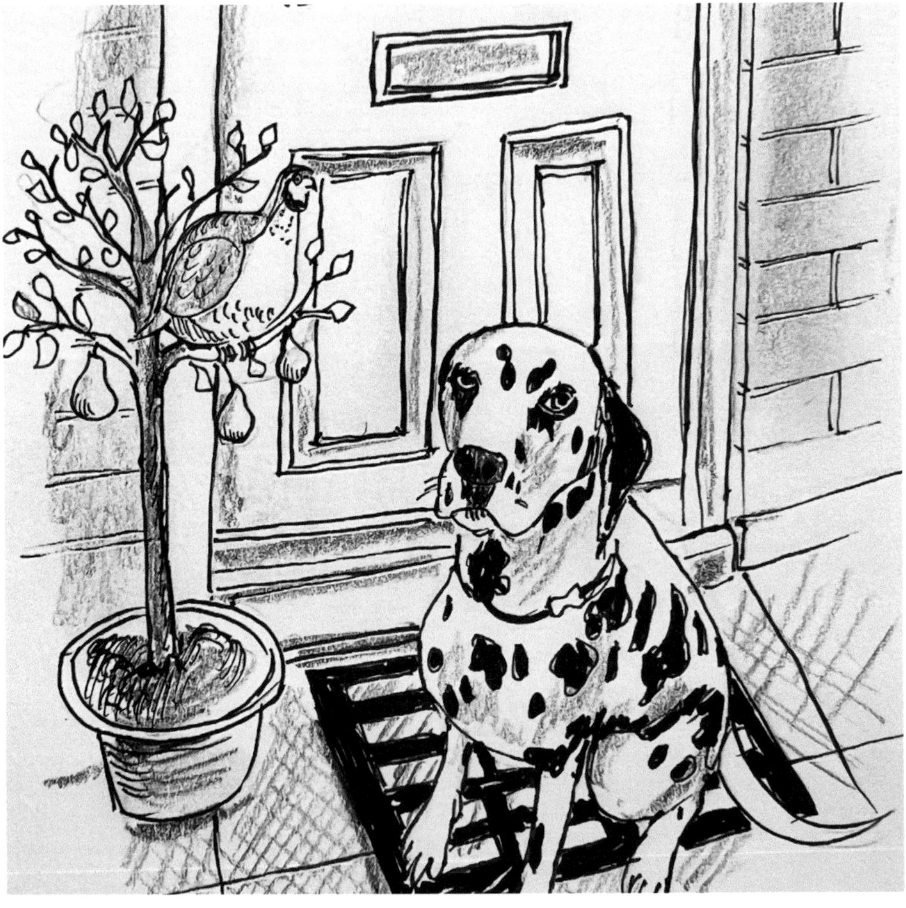

The first day

So knock me down with a feather. You'll never guess what I got
In my Christmas stocking this morning, a pear tree in a pot

And in the tree was a nestling, a funny looking bird
I had to look it up on Google. I guess surprised is just the word

I am now an owner of a partridge, who lives in the said pear tree
It was an unusual present, I say, and a present just for me

My true love signed the gift card, and don't get me wrong, I'm pleased
But I was hoping for a jacuzzi. Not a bird stuck in a tree

So just how long I keep it, before I can sell it on
Is a question for my conscience, I guess. Before the bird is gone

I might put the tree on the terrace. and hope the bird flies off
Or maybe a roasted dinner. Please don't tell my love

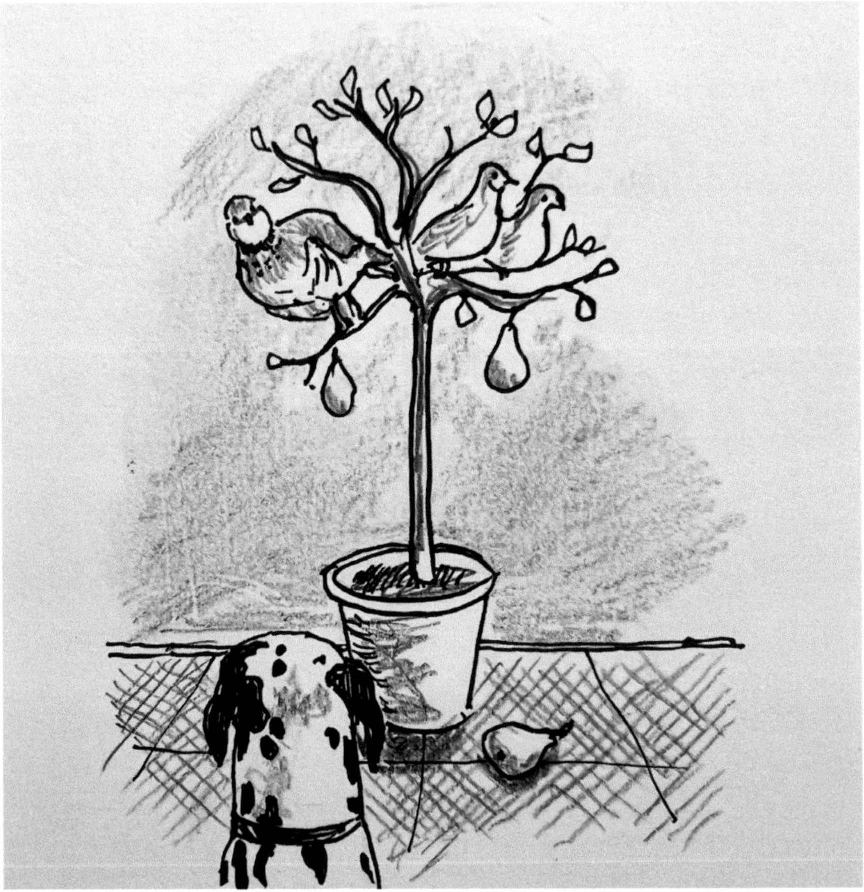

The second day

So there I was looking at my tree. With the partridge staring right back
When my true love said there's another gift. To be unwrapped from your Christmas sack

Well thoughts of the jacuzzi leapt to mind, as I pulled out another present
But what did I find instead of that? More flipping birds for advent

These two birds kept cooing at me. As if they knew my name
So now I have three birds and a tree. Just what is my true love's game?

So more birds, I said to her. I'm grateful for what I've got
But a partridge and two turtle doves. Is really quite a lot

And the pear tree now was full of life. With squawks and flapping wings
My Boxing Day with Bruce as well. Was a mixed up noisy thing

Hope I get some headphones

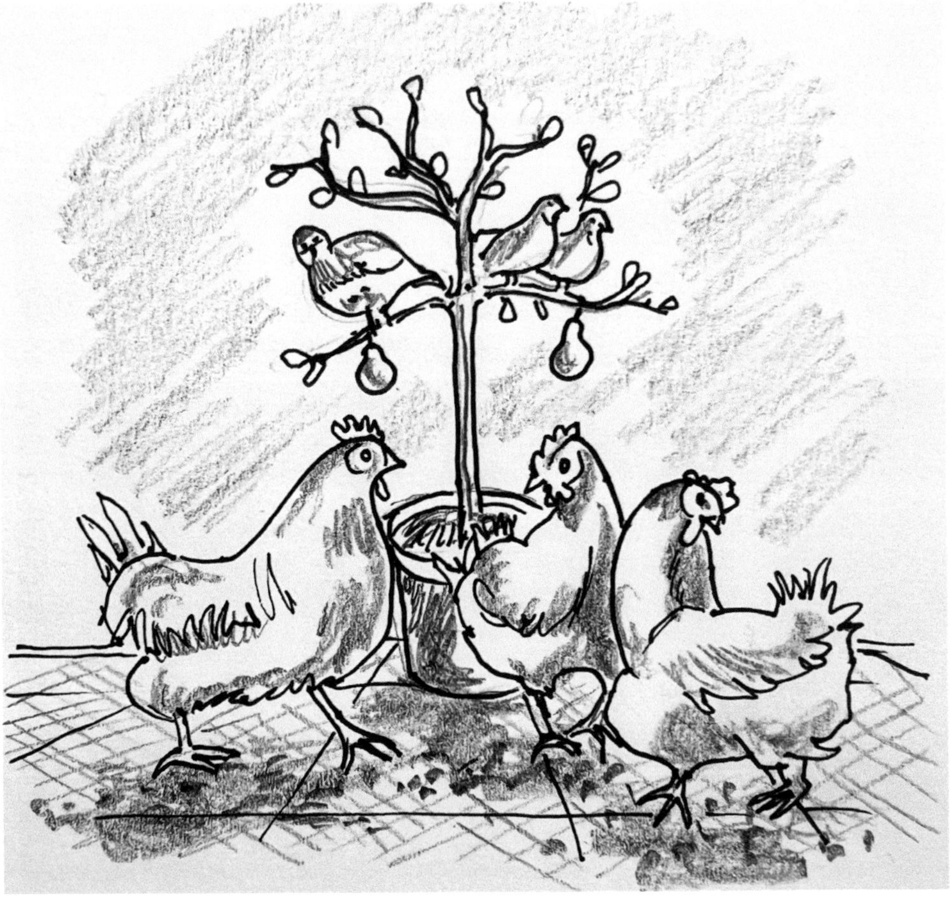

The third day

As I dozed the doorbell rang, and my true love stood outside
I've got another gift for you. Too much, I thought inside

But in she came with another gift. Finally, I thought
But if not the jacuzzi on my list. Maybe some socks that she had brought

I suspect that you know what's next on the list, and yes, you'd be right - spot on
More flipping birds for me again, my true love now long gone

I'm left with some French hens now. Three of them to be exact
So what with the other birds I've got. Bruce has run out the back

The pear tree is fully loaded, and I've got eggs for tea
I know I should be grateful. About what she's given me

Lots of bird poop

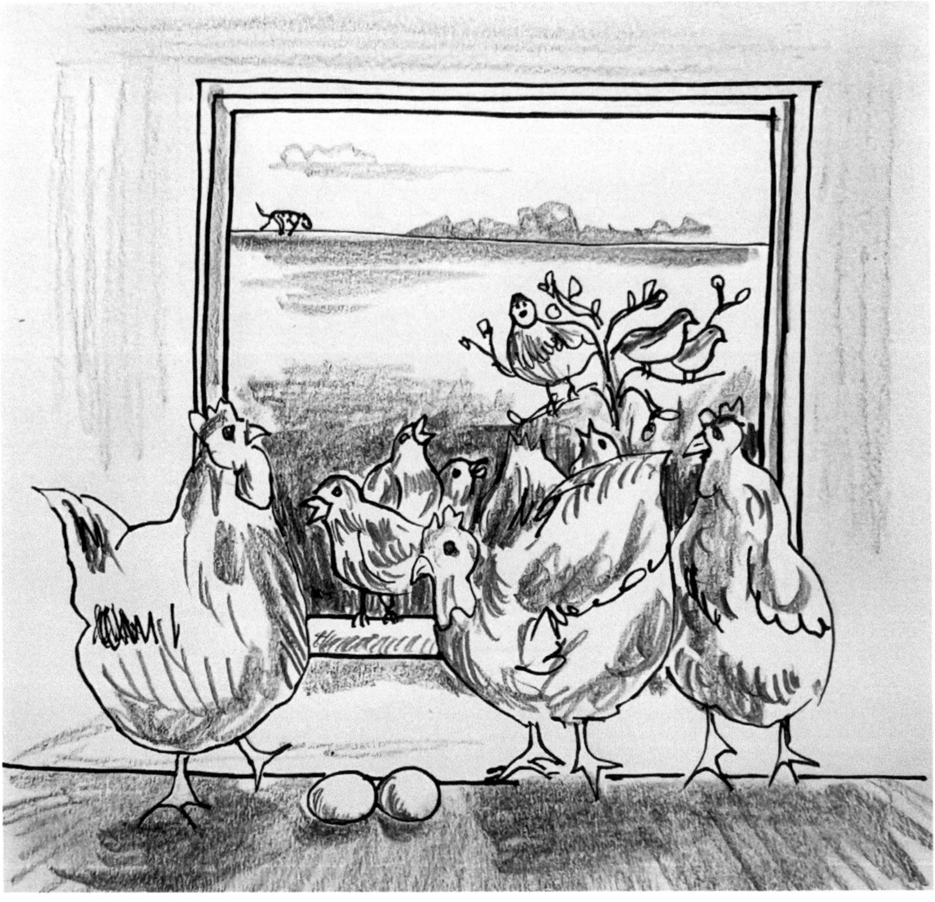

The fourth day

Oh please, oh please I think to myself. As the fourth day of Christmas begins
No more birds from my true love. In fact no more anything

But what does she send instead to me? Another batch of birds
Calling on me continuously. It's as if she hasn't heard

So now I have an aviary, to challenge any zoo
All thanks because of my true love. Just what can I do?

Get a new true love is an option. One not obsessed like her
In sending me so many flocks, and not frankincense and myrrh

I've reached the end of my tether. In fact, much more than that
Just like I'm running out of bird seed, no more the diplomat

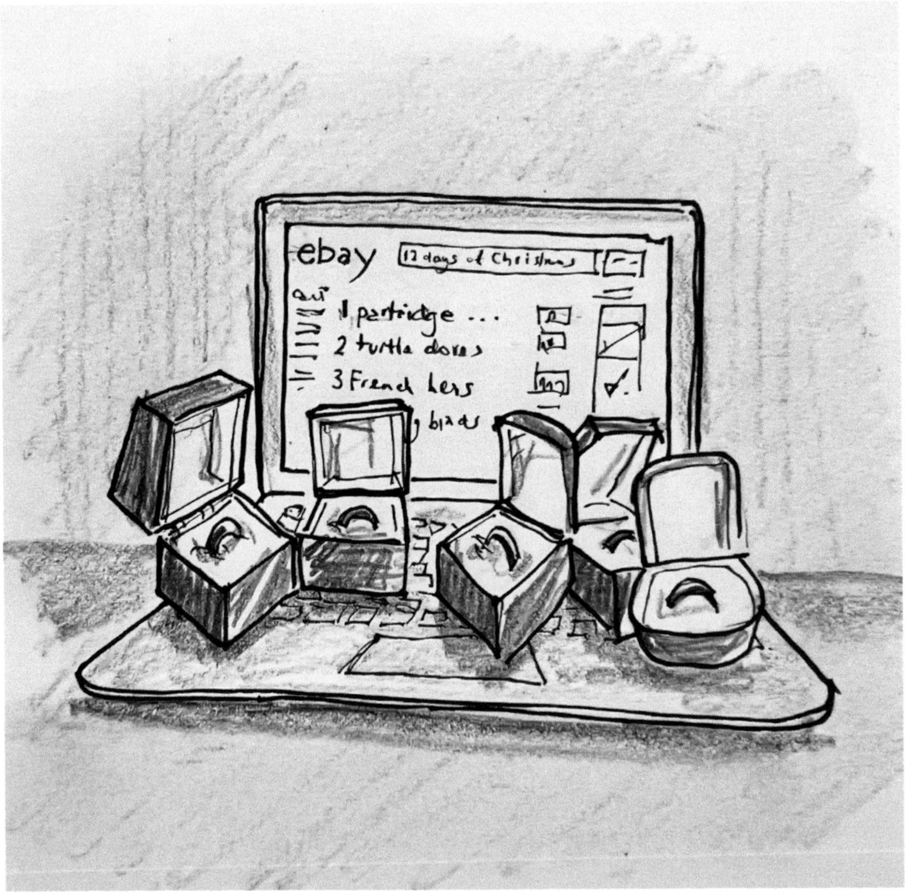
ebay
12 days of Christmas
1 partridge ...
2 turtle doves
3 French hens

The fifth day

Well knock me down with a feather. Just as I had lost my mind
My true love has gone and done it. Shown that she can be so kind

I'm blown away by these gold rings. I've got five of them as well
So now the birds don't matter, on eBay I will sell

So if you know of someone, who'd like a flock of birds
All different sorts, big and small. Like a great menagerie herd

I feel like Gollum from The Hobbit, with my precious five gold rings
I'm hanging onto these for sure. I understand how he loved these things

And now I'm feeling romantic. To my true love once again
All is forgiven, just a lovers' tiff. Even though she was a pain

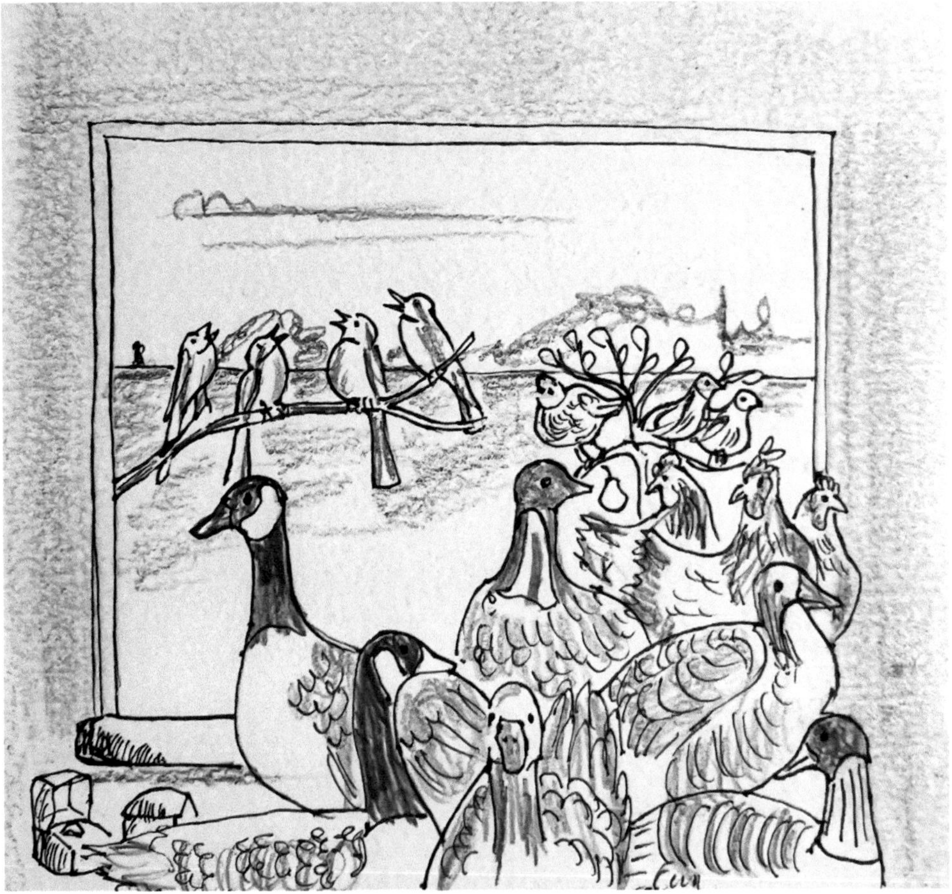

The sixth day

I'm barely able to speak now. My true love will soon be my ex
If she keeps bringing birds to me. I'm scared of what comes next

Six flipping geese are on my mat, can you imagine the scene?
That's sixteen birds in total now. I need so much caffeine

If I'm not going to strangle, my true love once and for all
It's so hard to be patient, as she threw this bird curveball

Take a deep breath and hope for the best. At least I've got the rings
And someone's contacted me on eBay. Oh joy I say and sing

You can have them for a bargain. Just make an offer please
In fact you can have them for nothing. I'm literally on my knees

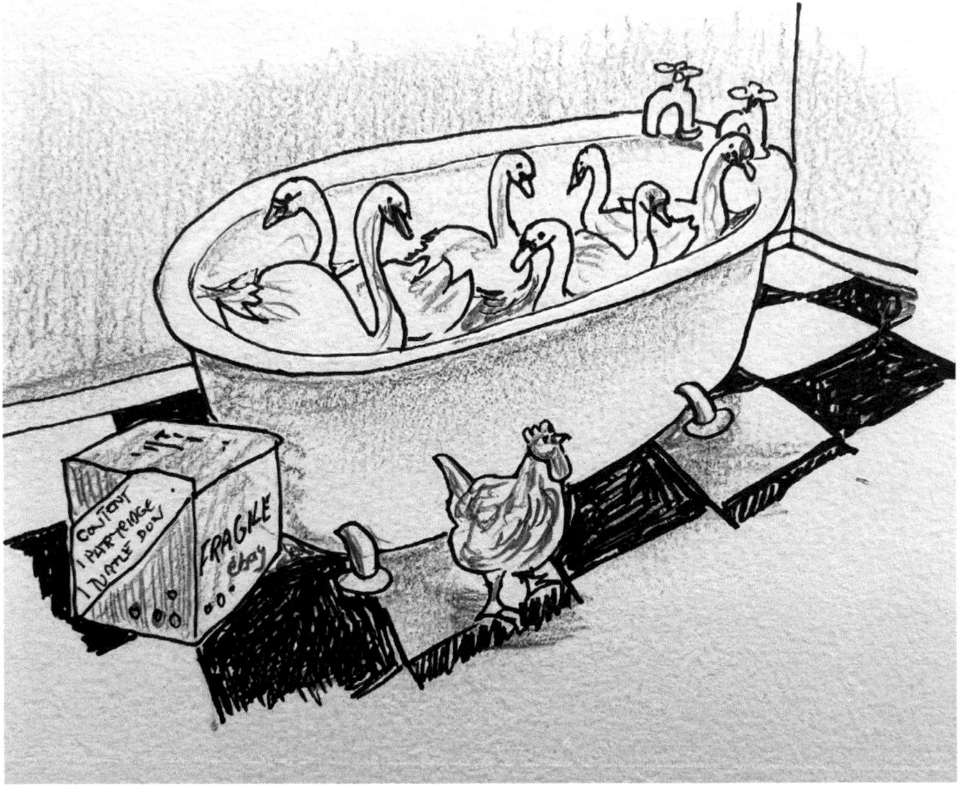
CONTENT
1 PARTRIDGE
1 TURTLE DOV
FRAGILE
ebay

The seventh day

I'm sorry but I can't find the words, for what I've just received
I've lost all sense of humour, it's your help I need

Whilst the eBayer took the partridge. and one of the turtle doves
I've got seven swans a'swimming. Sent from my annoying love

She must be mad and a bit insane, for her barking mad love gifts
I'm glad I didn't have a turkey, or I'd have more to shift

If you have any ideas, please, send me helpful clues
As what to do with these wretched birds. As I sit here feeling blue

I'm really scared about tomorrow, what's coming through that door
I'm like the bird man of Alcatraz now, more than I can endure

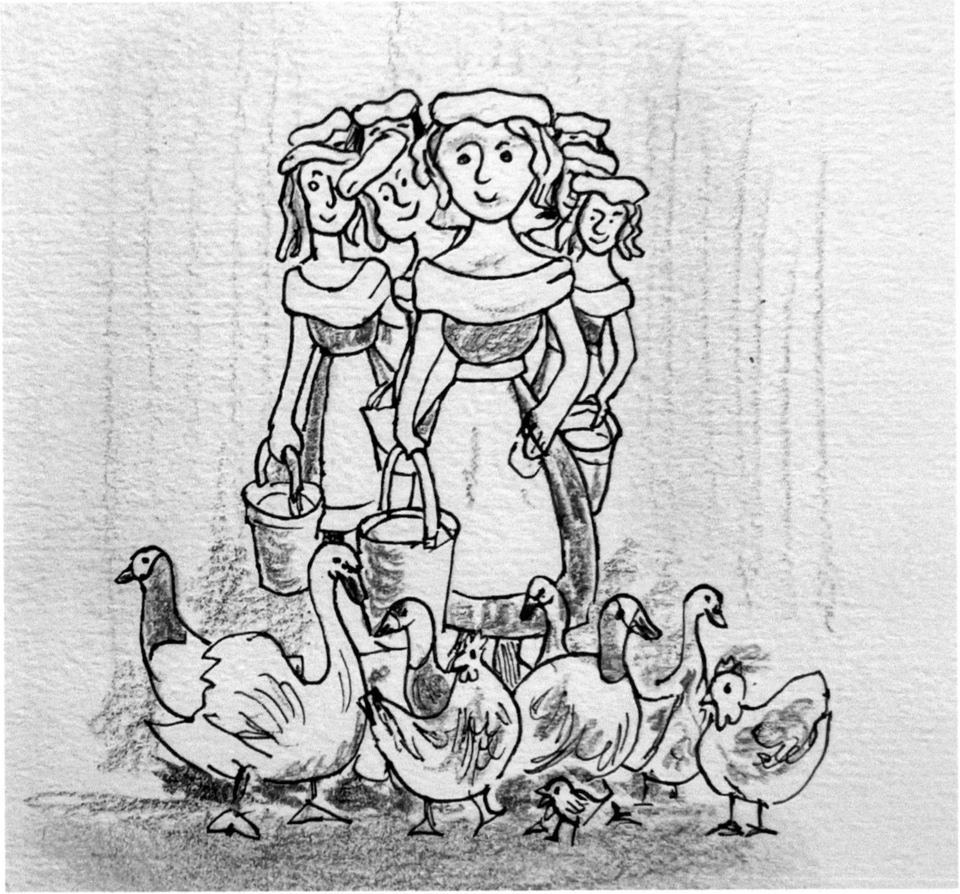

The eighth day

Il was expecting another flock of birds. from my evil once true love
But I must admit I was quite surprised, when I saw what turned up

Not one, not two, but eight maids in all. Here to milk the cows
And when I explained I'd only birds. As one they raised eyebrows

So I made them all a coffee, and we talked about a plan
To get rid of the birds and have a good time. Well there's eight and I'm a man

They didn't seem too keen on that, because they had a task
Even if there were no cows to milk, however nice I asked

And in my flat, I've got no room, and only two double beds
What was my true love thinking? Not birds but girls instead

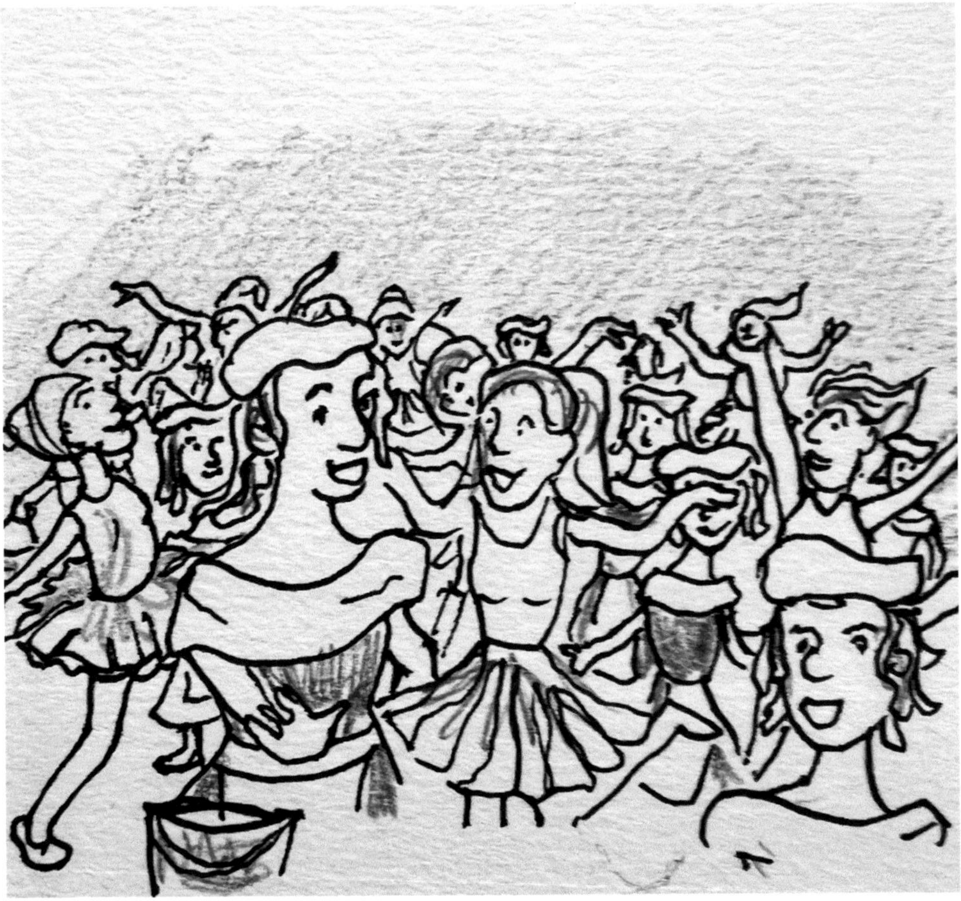

The ninth day

Well that was quite a night for me, I didn't get much sleep
So when the doorbell rang again, we were all laying in a heap

As if the maids were not enough. In came dancing girls
Nine of them I think I saw. Outnumbered that's for sure

I just sat down in the corner, not much that I could do
With ladies, maids, all chatting, I retreated to the loo

But in the loo the swans swam. Swimming round and round
And the turtle dove on the cistern. Let me explain the sound

With seventeen women chatting, and the bird noise in my ears
I couldn't hear myself think. My sanity I feared

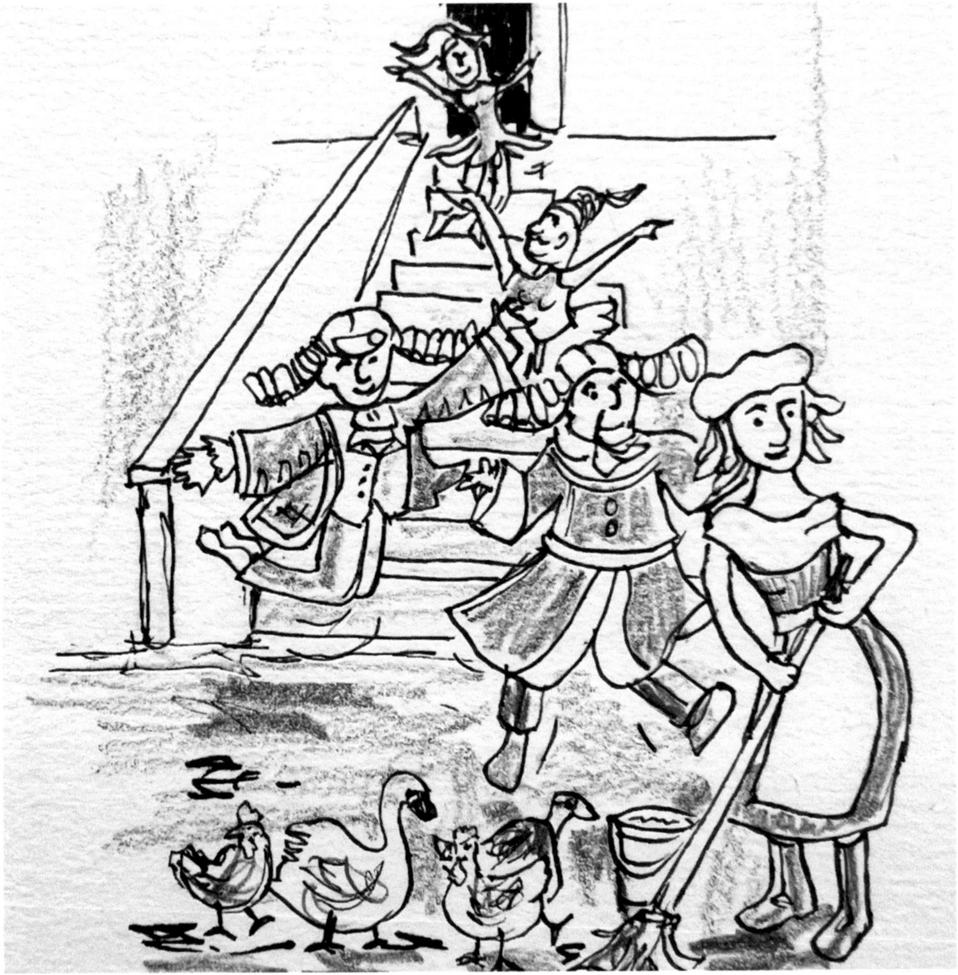

The tenth day

I lost the will to live long ago, so nothing surprises me now
Until it was the next gift arrived, I was blown away somehow

Ten lords all came in leaping, and some looked out of breath
Leaping around the ladies, and the flat that was a mess

The milking maids now cleaning, bird poop off the floor
So the lords shacked up with the dancers, and shut my bedroom door

The sound from the bedroom deafened, and drowned out the hissing swans
But the calling birds kept calling, I pray the end isn't long

Christmas must soon be over, just two more days to go
Hang on in there if you can. With my true love Christmas show

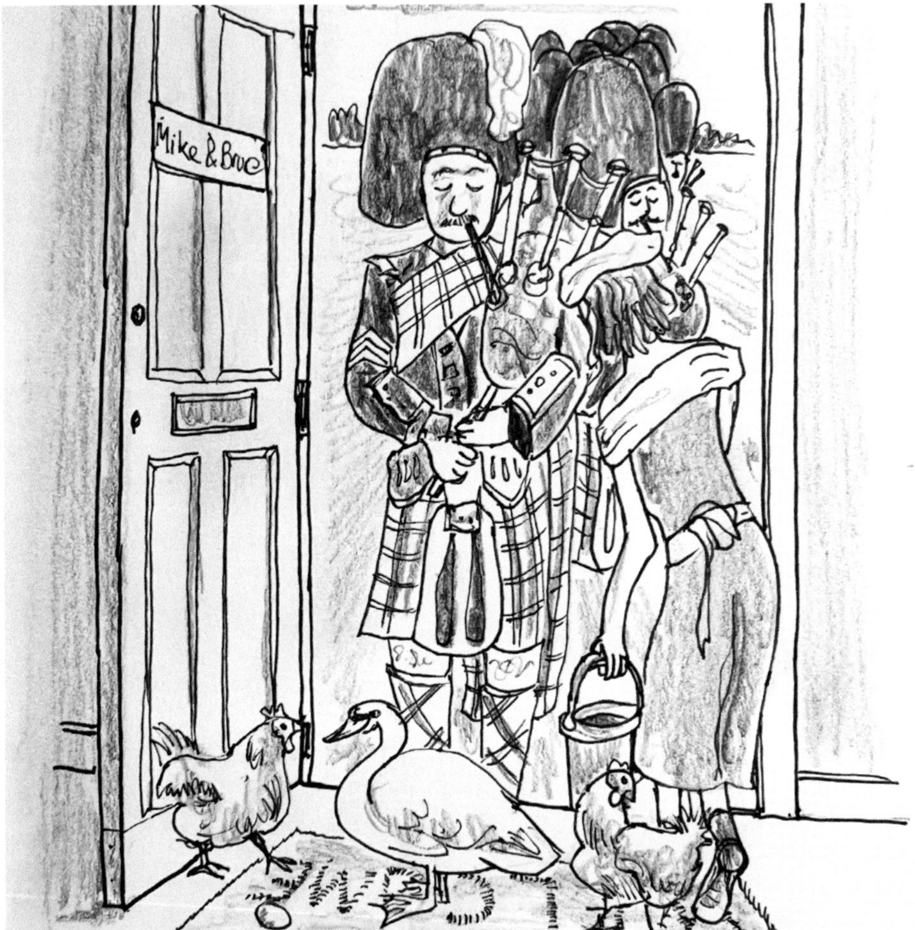
Mike & Bruc

The eleventh day

I could almost see the funny side, when the next lot burst inside
But my humour completely lost me, at the sound of the bagpipes

Eleven of them to be exact. With kilts swirling round and round
One of them accidentally trod on a goose, well that added to the sound

So what with the lords, the dancing girls, and the milking maids in the flat
It wasn't exactly a quiet time, I think you'd agree with that

This has been a Christmas to remember, and not one I want to repeat
At least not with the pipers, at least it was complete

was then that one of the milking maids. Reminded me there were twelve days in all
I sighed the sigh of a tired man, at the thought of tomorrow's call

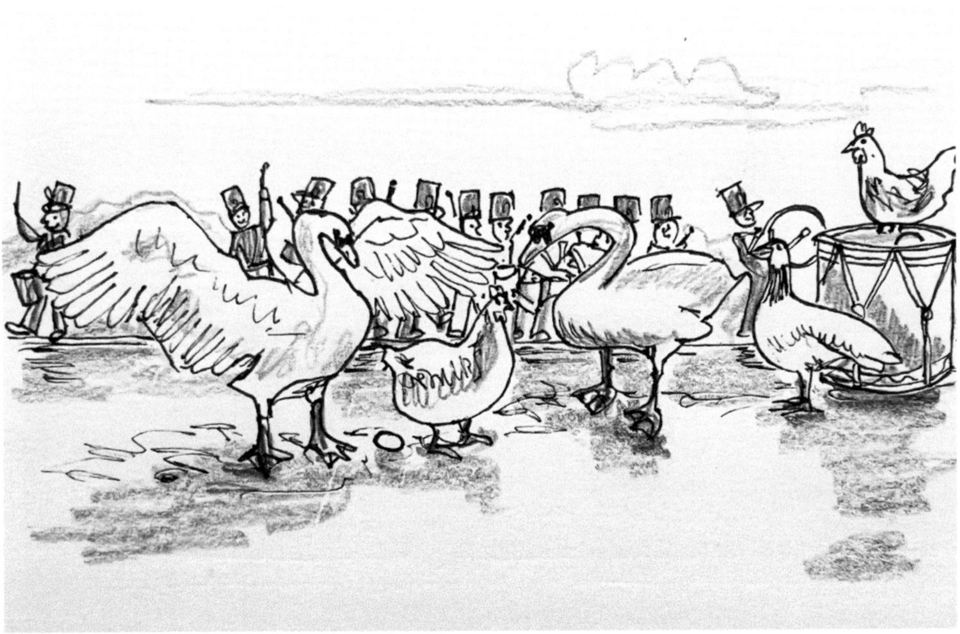

The twelfth day

At first, I couldn't hear them. For they were far away
Until they burst in through the door, banging drums to wake the day

Now one would have been too many, with what was going on
But twelve of them - what's that about? The drummers' drumming song

I tried to count all the things I'd got. From my evil once true love
She's obviously planned it for a while, raining gifts on me from above

I decided if I couldn't beat them, I'd join in all the fun
And as we all ate roasted birds, I looked back at what I'd done

Next time put a latch on my front door, and don't let anyone in
No birds no girls no leaping lords, and definitely no bagpipe din

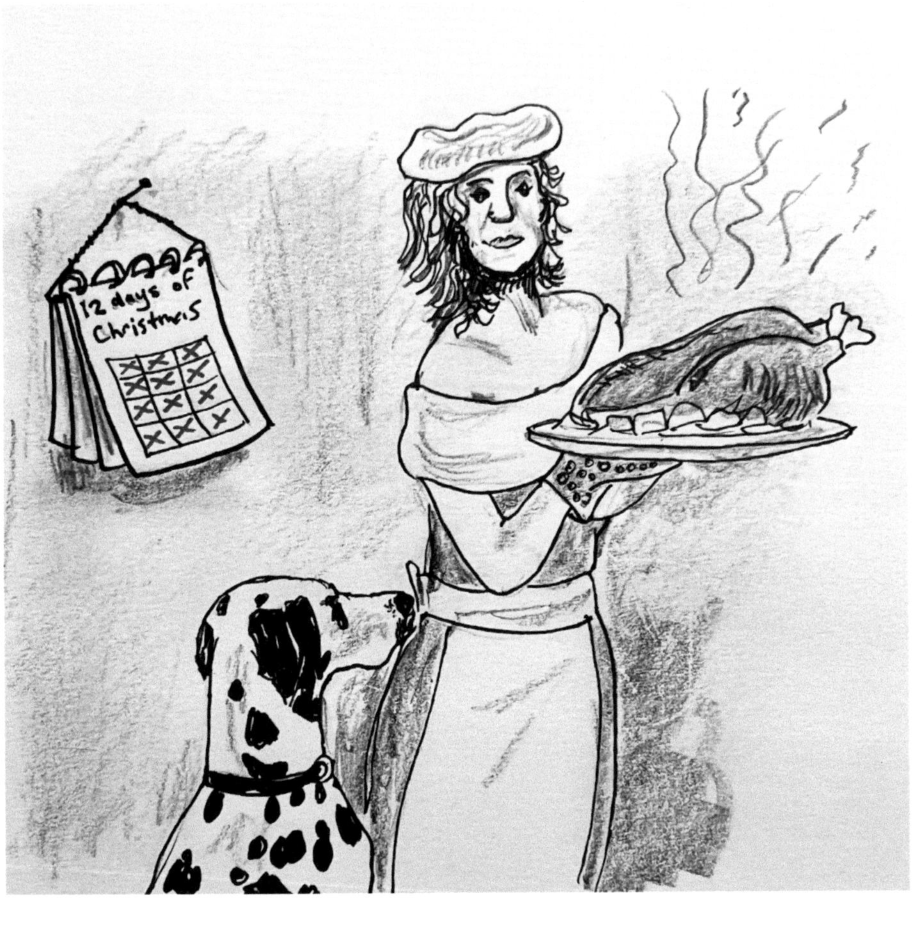
12 days of
Christmas

Finally it's over

And so my friends my Christmas is done. As the last one left the door
I've still lots of cleaning to do, I've kept a maid to do the floor

And now my once true love has gone, I've asked the maid to stay
I'll even get a cow outside, we can drink milk all through the day

My dog is back and sleeping now. Another new year starts
How was yours? Just like mine? Maybe just a little part

What's the message at Christmas, Goodwill to everyone
Well, I have had enough of that, especially now it's done

I'm having next year on my own, well maybe just with the maid
I don't want any presents please. So I'll build a big barricade

Have a great year

The casual poet

Mike Bourton, also known as the casual poet, has been writing his casual poems for the ast few years about whatever pops into his head. He often shares his stories with his dog, Bruce the Dalmatian, who clearly enjoys all the attention and treats it brings!

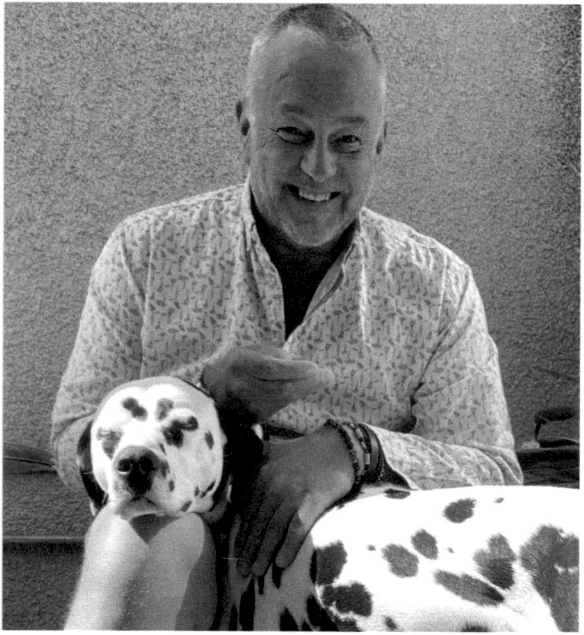

thecasualpoet.com